Woman'sDay

Wednesday Night is
Vegetarian

The Eat-Well Cookbook of Meals in a Hurry

Woman's Day

Wednesday Night is
Vegetarian

The Eat-Well Cookbook of Meals in a Hurry

filipacchi
publishing

Contents

MAIN DISHES • 56

CREDITS • 96

Rustic Summer Squash Tart

SKILLET & OVEN • SERVES 12 • TOTAL TIME: 1 HOUR 5 MINUTES

1 Tbsp extra-virgin olive oil

1 lb mixed summer squash (zucchini, yellow squash and pattypan), cut in ¼-in. rounds

2 shallots, thinly sliced

2 tsp chopped fresh thyme or marjoram, plus sprigs for garnish

1 tsp chopped garlic

Freshly ground pepper

1 refrigerated pie crust (from a 15-oz box of two)

4 oz Roquefort, Gorgonzola or other good-quality blue cheese

1 roasted yellow or red pepper (freshly roasted or from a jar), cut in strips

1 large plum tomato, sliced, seeds removed

1 large egg, beaten

1. Heat oil in a large nonstick skillet over medium heat. Add squash and shallots and cook, turning pieces as they start to color, 7 minutes or until crisp-tender. Remove from heat; stir in thyme, garlic and pepper to taste. Cool to room temperature.

2. Heat oven to 400°F. Line a baking sheet with parchment paper; unroll or unfold pie crust on the parchment. With a rolling pin, roll crust to a 13-in. round. Crumble ½ the cheese over crust to within 2 in. of edge. Arrange squash mixture, pepper strips and tomato slices on cheese; fold edge of the crust over filling and brush crust with egg.

3. Bake 35 to 40 minutes until pastry is golden. Slide tart, still on parchment, onto a wire rack. Crumble remaining cheese over top. Let cool before serving.

PER SERVING: **144 cal, 3 g pro, 12 g car, 1 g fiber, 9 g fat (4 g sat fat), 29 mg chol, 263 mg sod**

Plum Tomato Tart

SKILLET & OVEN • SERVES 6 • TOTAL TIME: 40 MINUTES

1 refrigerated pie crust (from a 15-oz box of two)

2 Tbsp olive oil

1 large onion, halved and thinly sliced

1½ tsp chopped fresh rosemary or ½ tsp dried

¼ tsp *each* salt and pepper

1 cup shredded fontina cheese

6 plum tomatoes, sliced

1. Position oven racks so one is in middle, the other in highest position. Heat oven to 450°F. Fit pie crust into a 9-in. tart pan with removable bottom; trim dough extending above pan. Lightly prick bottom with a fork.

2. Place on a baking sheet and bake crust on middle oven rack 9 to 11 minutes until golden.

3. Meanwhile, heat 1 Tbsp oil in a large nonstick skillet over medium heat. Add onion, rosemary and ⅛ tsp each salt and pepper. Cook, stirring occasionally, 10 minutes or until golden.

4. Transfer tart pan to baking sheet. Heat broiler. Immediately sprinkle cheese over bottom of crust and top with onion. Arrange tomatoes in slightly overlapping concentric circles on top to cover. Brush with 1 Tbsp oil; sprinkle with remaining salt and pepper. Cover crust edge with foil to prevent scorching.

5. Broil 8 to 12 minutes until tomatoes just begin to char. Let stand 5 minutes. Carefully push tart bottom through sides; place on serving plate. Serve warm or at room temperature.

PER SERVING: **305 cal, 6 g pro, 25 g car, 2 g fiber, 20 g fat (8 g sat fat), 28 mg chol, 383 mg sod**

Cheddar-Vegetable Quiche

OVEN • SERVES 6 • TOTAL TIME: 1 HOUR

1 refrigerated pie crust (from a 15-oz box of two)

1 bag (24 oz) frozen broccoli, carrots, cauliflower and Cheddar cheese sauce

1 carton (15 oz) cheese and chive Egg Beaters

GARNISH: chives

1. Heat oven to 400°F. Lightly coat a 9-in. pie plate with nonstick spray.

2. Fit crust into pie plate, turn edges under and crimp or flute. Prick crust in several places. Press a sheet of foil directly on crust. Bake 12 to 14 minutes until edges are lightly browned. Remove foil; cool crust on a wire rack while preparing vegetables.

3. Microwave vegetables and cheese sauce as bag directs. Stir in Egg Beaters and pour into crust.

4. Bake 15 minutes; reduce heat to 350°F and bake 20 to 25 minutes until a knife inserted near center of quiche comes out clean. If desired, garnish with chives.

PER SERVING: **251 cal, 9 g pro, 26 g car, 2 g fiber, 12 g fat (6 g sat fat), 13 mg chol, 735 mg sod**

Sweet Onion & Cheddar Pizza

GRILL • SERVES 6 • TOTAL TIME: 25 MINUTES

1 tube (13.8 oz) refrigerated pizza crust

1 medium sweet onion, cut in ½-in.-thick slices

Nonstick cooking spray

1 can (8 oz) tomato sauce

1¼ cups shredded Cheddar cheese

GARNISH: chopped parsley

1. Heat outdoor grill. Line a baking sheet with nonstick foil. Unroll dough on foil; press into a 16 x 10-in. rectangle. Coat dough and onion with nonstick spray.

2. Grill onion 10 minutes, turning slices as needed, until tender. Remove; cut into bite-size pieces. Invert dough on grill; peel off foil. Grill 1 minute until bottom is lightly browned. Turn crust over and spread with sauce; top with onion and cheese. Cover and grill 2 minutes until cheese melts; remove. Sprinkle with parsley; cut in 12 pieces.

PER SERVING: **273 cal, 13 g pro, 34 g car, 2 g fiber, 10 g fat (5 g sat fat), 25 mg chol, 1,013 mg sod**

Grilled Eggplant Parmesan Pizza

GRILL • SERVES 4 • TOTAL TIME: 23 MINUTES

4 baby eggplants, cut crosswise in ½-in.-thick slices

4 pocketless pitas

Olive-oil nonstick cooking spray

1 cup bottled marinara sauce

1 cup *each* part-skim ricotta and shredded part-skim mozzarella cheese

2 Tbsp grated Parmesan cheese

GARNISH: chopped fresh basil leaves

1. Heat outdoor grill. Coat eggplant and pitas with nonstick spray.

2. Grill eggplant 10 minutes, turning as needed, until tender; remove. Grill pitas 1 minute until bottoms are lightly charred. Remove to a platter; spread grilled sides with the sauce, then top with eggplant, dollop of ricotta, mozzarella and Parmesan.

3. Return to grill. Cover and grill 1 to 2 minutes until cheeses melt. Remove; cut each in 4 wedges. Garnish with basil.

PER SERVING: **427 cal, 23 g pro, 53 g car, 4 g fiber, 15 g fat (7 g sat fat), 37 mg chol, 976 mg sod**

Grilled Tuscan Pizzas

GRILL • SERVES 4 • TOTAL TIME: 15 MINUTES

4 Mediterranean-style flatbreads
or pocketless pitas

2 tsp oil

1 tub (10½ oz) Tuscan Bruschetta

1 cup shredded mozzarella cheese

GARNISH: torn fresh basil leaves

1. Heat outdoor grill. Brush flatbreads with oil and place directly on grill. Grill 1½ to 2 minutes or until bottoms are lightly charred. Place charred side up on baking sheet. Spread top of each with scant ⅓ cup bruschetta, then top each with ¼ cup mozzarella.

2. Return to grill. Close cover and grill 1 to 2 minutes until bottoms are lightly charred and toppings warm. Garnish with torn basil leaves if desired. Cut in wedges.

PER SERVING: **337 cal, 12 g pro, 39 g car, 4 g fiber, 15 g fat (5 g sat fat), 15 mg chol, 698 mg sod**

VARIATION
Instead of Bruschetta, spread flatbreads with basil pesto. Top with baby arugula leaves and shaved Parmesan.

Open-Face Zucchini Sandwiches

SKILLET • SERVES 4 • TOTAL TIME: 15 MINUTES

1 Tbsp olive oil

2 zucchinis, sliced ¼ in. thick

4 large slices Italian bread (from center of a round loaf), toasted

1 large beefsteak tomato, cut in 8 slices

¾ cup shredded mozzarella and Asiago cheese with roasted garlic or ¾ cup shredded mozzarella cheese

½ tsp dried oregano

¼ tsp *each* salt and pepper

½ cup fresh basil leaves

1. Heat oil in a large nonstick skillet. Add zucchini; cook over high heat 4 minutes, turning once, until golden and tender.

2. Meanwhile, top each slice of bread with 2 slices tomato and 3 Tbsp cheese.

3. Sprinkle zucchini with oregano, salt and pepper; lift from skillet with a slotted spoon onto the bread. Scatter basil over top.

PER SERVING: **285 cal, 12 g pro, 36 g car, 4 g fiber, 10 g fat (4 g sat fat), 15 mg chol, 650 mg sod**

Asian Bean Burgers

SKILLET • SERVES 4 • TOTAL TIME: 18 MINUTES

BURGERS

2 cans (15 to 16 oz each)
red kidney beans, rinsed

½ cup plain dry bread crumbs

⅓ cup minced scallions

1 large egg

1 Tbsp lite soy sauce

1 tsp *each* ground ginger and
minced garlic

1 Tbsp oil

SAUCE

¼ cup light mayonnaise

1 Tbsp prepared white horseradish

1 Tbsp minced scallions

1 tsp lite soy sauce

4 hamburger buns

Lettuce and sliced tomato
and cucumber

1. BURGERS: Mash beans in a medium bowl with a potato masher or fork. Stir in remaining burger ingredients until well blended. Form into 4 patties.

2. Heat oil in a large nonstick skillet over medium heat. Cook patties 3 to 4 minutes per side until heated through and crusty and internal temperature registers 160°F on an instant-read thermometer inserted from side into middle.

3. SAUCE: Mix ingredients in a small bowl.

4. Serve the burgers on buns with lettuce, tomato, cucumber and the sauce.

PER SERVING **(without lettuce, tomato and cucumber): 436 cal, 18 g pro, 59 g car, 10 g fiber, 14 g fat (2 g sat fat), 58 mg chol, 958 mg sod**

Open-Face Portobello "Burgers"

6 portobello mushrooms caps, wiped with a damp paper towel

1 large red onion, cut in six ¼-in.-thick slices (slices slightly smaller than mushroom caps)

6 Tbsp extra-virgin olive oil, plus extra for drizzling

1 loaf ciabatta bread, halved horizontally and cut in 6 pieces, or six 4-in.-square pieces herbed focaccia bread

2 Tbsp balsamic vinegar

1 clove garlic, crushed through a press

½ tsp *each* salt and freshly ground pepper

12 oz fontina cheese, cut in 6 slices

18 large fresh basil leaves, plus extra for garnish

1 large beefsteak tomato, cut in 6 thick slices

1. Heat outdoor grill. Brush mushrooms and onion slices with 3 Tbsp oil. Grill onion and mushrooms, gill sides down, 12 minutes, turning after 6 minutes, or until onion and mushrooms are crisp-tender.

2. Meanwhile, brush cut sides of bread with 2 Tbsp oil. Grill, cut sides down, 2 minutes or just until lightly toasted. Transfer to a platter; cover with foil to keep warm.

3. Mix remaining 1 Tbsp oil, vinegar, garlic, and ¼ tsp each salt and pepper. Using a spatula, place an onion slice in the cavity of each mushroom and brush with vinegar mixture. Top each with cheese, 3 basil leaves and 1 tomato slice. Drizzle tomatoes with oil, if desired, and sprinkle with remaining salt and pepper.

4. Cover grill and cook 2 to 3 minutes or until cheese is melted and soft.

5. Place a mushroom "burger" on each piece of grilled bread. Cut a few basil leaves in thin strips and sprinkle on burgers for garnish.

PER SERVING: **516 cal, 22 g pro, 43 g car, 3 g fiber, 32 g fat (13 g sat fat), 65 mg chol, 1027 mg sod**

Pita Panini with Arugula Salad

GRILL • SERVES 4 • TOTAL TIME: 10 MINUTES

4 regular-size pitas

½ cup refrigerated reduced-fat pesto

1 jar (12 oz) roasted red peppers, well-drained

2 cups shredded part-skim mozzarella cheese

1 medium onion, cut in ½-in.-thick slices

Nonstick cooking spray

1 bag (5 oz) baby arugula

1 large tomato, cut in wedges

3 Tbsp reduced-fat balsamic vinaigrette

1. Heat a ridged stovetop grill pan or outdoor grill.

2. Meanwhile, make panini: For each, split 1 pita and spread the rough side of a half with 2 Tbsp pesto. Top with ¼ of the peppers and ½ cup cheese. Cover with the other half of the pita, smooth side up.

3. Lightly coat both sides of panini and onion slices with nonstick spray. Grill 4 to 5 minutes, turning once or twice, until cheese melts and onion slices are charred and crisp-tender.

4. Meanwhile, toss arugula, tomato and dressing in a large bowl. Stir in charred onion. Serve with panini.

PER SERVING: **474 cal, 23 g pro, 46 g car, 4 g fiber, 21 g fat (9 g sat fat), 36 mg chol, 1,286 mg sod**

Two-Bean Sloppy Joes

BEAN MIXTURE

1 can *each* (15 to 16 oz) black-eyed peas and red kidney beans, rinsed

1½ cups bottled marinara sauce

1 can (14½ oz) no-salt-added diced tomatoes in juice, drained

½ cup *each* frozen cut green beans and chopped green bell pepper

1 Tbsp Worcestershire sauce

2 tsp red wine vinegar

1½ tsp chili powder

4 split seeded kaiser or hamburger rolls, toasted

1. BEAN MIXTURE: Bring all ingredients to a boil in a 10- or 12-in. nonstick skillet over medium-high heat. Reduce heat, partially cover skillet and simmer, stirring occasionally, 10 to 15 minutes until green pepper is tender.

2. Spoon onto roll bottoms; replace tops.

PER SERVING: **433 cal, 20 g pro, 75 g car, 9 g fiber, 8 g fat (1 g sat fat), 0 mg chol, 1,429 mg sod**

The perfect accompaniment? Coleslaw.

Bean & Vegetable Burritos

SKILLET • SERVES 5 • TOTAL TIME: 30 MINUTES

5 burrito-size flour tortillas, preferably flavored (we used spinach with garlic and pesto)

FILLING

2 tsp oil

1 zucchini, diced

1⅔ cups sliced onion

2½ tsp salt-free chili powder

1 bag (10 oz) fresh spinach, rinsed, dried and coarsely chopped

1 can (15 to 16 oz) black beans, rinsed

1 can (11 oz) corn, drained

ACCOMPANIMENTS: reduced-fat sour cream, lime wedges and salsa

1. Warm tortillas as package directs.

2. FILLING: Heat oil in a large nonstick skillet over medium-high heat. Add zucchini and onions. Sauté 6 minutes or until browned and tender. Add chili powder; stir 30 seconds or until fragrant. Add spinach a few handfuls at a time, adding more as it cooks down. Stir in beans and corn; heat through.

3. FOR EACH BURRITO: Spoon about 1 cup filling on bottom third of tortilla. Roll bottom over filling, turn in sides and continue to roll up. Place seam side down on serving platter. Serve accompaniments in small bowls alongside.

PER SERVING (without accompaniments): 364 cal, 13 g pro, 62 g car, 11 g fiber, 8 g fat (1 g sat fat), 0 mg chol, 891 mg sod

Crispy Skillet Burritos

SKILLET • SERVES 4 • TOTAL TIME: 23 MINUTES

1 cup uncooked quick-cooking rice

1 can (15 to 16 oz) black beans, rinsed

½ cup *each* salsa and shredded reduced-fat Cheddar cheese

¼ cup *each* chopped cilantro and scallions

½ tsp ground cumin

4 burrito-size flour tortillas

Nonstick cooking spray

SERVE WITH: salsa and sour cream

1. Prepare rice as package directs. Stir in next four ingredients.

2. Spoon 1 cup mixture on each tortilla. Roll, tucking in two opposite sides to enclose filling. Coat with nonstick spray.

3. Heat a large nonstick skillet over medium heat. Add burritos, seam side down, and cook 5 minutes, turning as needed, until browned. Reduce heat to low, cover and cook 2 minutes to heat filling.

PER SERVING: **503 cal, 18 g pro, 86 g car, 6 g fiber, 10 g fat (3 g sat fat), 10 mg chol, 997 mg sod**

Portobello Fajitas

SKILLETS • SERVES 4 • TOTAL TIME: 14 MINUTES

2 tsp oil

4 large portobello mushroom caps, wiped with a damp paper towel

2 green bell peppers, sliced

1 medium onion, sliced

1 pkt (1.12 oz) fajita seasoning

8 lettuce leaves

8 soft tacos-size flour tortillas, warmed

SERVE WITH: sour cream and cilantro sprigs

1. Heat 1 tsp oil in each of two skillets over medium-high heat. Add mushrooms to one skillet, peppers and onion to the other.

2. Cook 6 minutes, turning mushrooms and stirring pepper mixture occasionally, until firm-tender. Remove mushrooms to cutting board. Stir seasoning and ⅓ cup water into pepper mixture. Cook 1 minute until saucy.

3. Slice mushrooms. Roll up with peppers and onions in warmed lettuce-lined tortillas. Serve with sour cream and cilantro.

PER SERVING: **302 cal, 10 g pro, 55 g car, 6 g fiber, 7 g fat (1 g sat fat), 0 mg chol, 1,023 mg sod**

Bean, Spinach & Corn Quesadillas

OVEN • SERVES 8 • TOTAL TIME: 25 MINUTES

6 fajita-size flour tortillas

1 cup canned black beans, rinsed

½ can chipotle pepper in adobo sauce, minced

1 pkg (10 oz) frozen chopped spinach, thawed and squeezed dry

1 cup canned, frozen or fresh corn kernels

1 cup shredded reduced-fat Monterey Jack cheese

1½ cups bottled tomato salsa

1 cup fat-free sour cream

1. Heat oven to 400°F.

2. Coat a large baking sheet with nonstick spray. Lay tortillas in a single layer on work surface. Mash beans with chipotle pepper. Spread on half of each tortilla. Top beans with spinach, corn and cheese. Fold tortillas in half, pressing top half firmly on filling.

3. Bake 10 minutes or until golden on bottom. Flip over, bake 5 minutes more until crisp. Cut each in 4 wedges. Serve topped with salsa and sour cream.

PER SERVING: **224 cal, 12 g pro, 32 g car, 3 g fiber, 5 g fat (2 g sat fat), 13 mg chol, 719 mg sod**

Asian Sesame-Apple Slaw

SERVES 8 • TOTAL TIME: 35 MINUTES

¼ cup seasoned rice vinegar

2 Tbsp dark sesame oil

1 Tbsp honey

½ tsp salt

1 jalapeño or serrano pepper, seeded and minced (2 tsp)

1 *each* Gala, Golden Delicious and Granny Smith apple, halved, cored and thinly sliced

8 cups finely shredded Napa cabbage

1 red bell pepper, seeded, cut in thin strips

½ seedless cucumber, cut in thin strips

3 scallions, thinly sliced

¾ cup cilantro

2 Tbsp toasted sesame seeds

1 container (3 oz) radish sprouts

1. In a large bowl, whisk vinegar, oil, honey, salt and chile pepper until blended. Add apple slices and toss to coat.

2. Add remaining ingredients, except radish sprouts, and toss to coat (slaw can be made up to 4 hours ahead and refrigerated). Just before serving, scatter radish sprouts over the slaw. Gently toss.

PER SERVING: **125 cal, 2 g pro, 19 g car, 5 g fiber, 5 g fat (1 g sat fat), 0 mg chol, 424 mg sod**

Edamame Salad

SERVES 4 • TOTAL TIME: 15 MINUTES

1 bag (16 oz) frozen, shelled edamame

1 can (11 oz) corn or 1½ cups cooked fresh corn kernels

4 to 6 medium radishes, cut in half and thinly sliced

¼ cup chopped cilantro

¼ cup sliced scallions

½ cup rice or wine vinegar

1 Tbsp vegetable oil

1 Tbsp wasabi powder

1 tsp minced garlic

1. Cook edamame as package directs, omitting salt. Cool under cold running water; drain well. Toss with corn, radishes, cilantro and scallions in a large bowl.

2. Whisk vinegar, oil, wasabi powder and garlic in a small bowl; toss with edamame mixture. Serve at room temperature or chill.

PER SERVING: **272 cal, 17 g pro, 27 g car, 6 g fiber, 12 g fat (1 g sat fat), 0 mg chol, 156 mg sod**

Very Veggie Pasta Salad

SERVES 4 • TOTAL TIME: 20 MINUTES

1 large ripe tomato, cut in bite-size pieces

1 small red onion, thinly sliced

1 cup thinly sliced red bell pepper

⅓ cup balsamic vinaigrette

1 pkg (16 oz) frozen cheese tortellini

4 cups broccoli florets

½ cup chopped fresh basil

1 bag (5 oz) spring lettuce mixture

1 cup smoked or regular mozzarella cheese, cut in small cubes

1. Bring a large pot of lightly salted water to a boil. Meanwhile, combine tomato, onion, pepper and dressing in a large bowl. Leave at room temperature.

2. Add tortellini to boiling water; cook as package directs, adding broccoli to pot 5 minutes before tortellini is done.

3. Drain; rinse under running cold water. Add to tomato mixture; add basil and toss to mix.

4. Arrange 1 cup lettuce on each of four plates. Top with tortellini mixture and mozzarella.

PER SERVING: **547 cal, 26 g pro, 68 g car, 7 g fiber, 21 g fat (9 g sat fat), 73 mg chol, 902 mg sod**

Tomato-Basil Pasta Salad

SERVES 8 • TOTAL TIME: 1 HOUR

3 large ripe tomatoes, coarsely chopped

⅓ cup chopped red onion

¼ cup extra-virgin olive oil

2 Tbsp red wine vinegar

1 tsp minced garlic

⅓ tsp *each* salt and pepper

¼ tsp dried oregano

12 oz fusilli pasta (or your favorite pasta)

1 cup fresh basil leaves, cut into thin strips

1. Put tomatoes, onion, oil, vinegar, garlic, salt, pepper and oregano in a large bowl; toss. Let stand at room temperature at least 30 minutes or until tomatoes release their juices, tossing occasionally.

2. Cook pasta in a large pot of lightly salted boiling water as package directs. Drain and add to bowl with tomatoes; lightly toss. Let come to room temperature. Add basil; toss. Serve or refrigerate up to 1 day.

PER SERVING: **242 cal, 7 g pro, 36 g car, 3 g fiber, 8 g fat (1 g sat fat), 0 mg chol, 152 mg sod**

Beet, Orange & Walnut Salad

OVEN • SERVES 6 • TOTAL TIME: 1 HOUR 30 MINUTES

DRESSING

¼ cup orange juice

2½ Tbsp olive oil

1 Tbsp lemon juice

1½ tsp sugar

¼ tsp *each* salt and pepper

SALAD

2 bunches small beets, leaves and stems removed, beets scrubbed

⅛ tsp *each* salt and pepper

2 navel oranges

1 small head green-leaf lettuce, leaves separated

¼ cup walnuts, toasted and coarsely chopped

GARNISH: chives

1. DRESSING: Shake all ingredients in a covered jar; refrigerate.

2. SALAD: Heat oven to 375°F. Line a rimmed baking sheet with nonstick foil. Add beets; cover pan with foil.

3. Roast 1¼ hours or until beets are tender. Meanwhile, cut peel and pith from oranges; slice. When beets are cool enough to handle, rub off skins with your fingers and slice. Toss in large bowl with ¼ cup dressing and the salt and pepper.

4. Arrange lettuce leaves, beet and orange slices on a large serving platter or individual salad plates. Drizzle with remaining dressing; sprinkle with walnuts and garnish with chives.

PER SERVING: **150 cal, 3 g pro, 18 g car, 4 g fiber, 9 g fat (1 g sat fat), 0 mg chol, 221 mg sod**

Spring Greens with Parmesan Crisps

OVEN • SERVES 8 • TOTAL TIME: 20 MINUTES

½ cup shredded Parmesan cheese

2½ Tbsp lemon juice

2 tsp Dijon mustard

¼ tsp pepper

¼ cup olive oil

2 heads Boston lettuce, torn into bite-size pieces (6 to 8 cups)

2 cups torn frisée (curly endive)

2 Tbsp *each* snipped chives and dill

1. Heat oven to 375°F. Line a baking sheet with nonstick foil. Spoon Parmesan onto lined sheet in eight 3-in. rounds, 1 Tbsp each, 1 in. apart. Bake 6 to 7 minutes until golden. To curl, remove crisps from foil with tongs while hot. Drape over a rolling pin until cool enough to retain curve.

2. Whisk lemon juice, mustard and pepper in small bowl; slowly whisk in oil until blended.

3. Toss lettuce and frisée with herbs and dressing. Serve with crisps.

PER SERVING: **92 cal, 3 g pro, 3 g car, 1 g fiber, 8 g fat (2 g sat fat), 4 mg chol, 122 mg sod**

PLAN AHEAD: You can prepare the dressing and crisps two days before serving.

Chilled Carrot-Ginger Soup

FOOD PROCESSOR OR BLENDER • SERVES 4 • TOTAL TIME: 35 MINUTES (PLUS CHILLING)

2 cups water

1½ lb peeled baby carrots

4 tsp minced fresh ginger

1½ cups buttermilk

¼ tsp salt

1. Bring water to a boil in medium saucepan. Add carrots and ginger; cook, covered, over medium-low heat 25 minutes or until tender; chill in covered saucepan.

2. Purée carrots and liquid in food processor or blender until smooth. Pour into a bowl; stir in buttermilk and salt. Swirl in a little extra buttermilk to decorate.

PER SERVING: 103 cal, 5 g pro, 19 g car, 3 g fiber,
2 g fat (1 g sat fat), 3 mg chol, 301 mg sod

Nectarine & Tomato Soup

SERVES 4 • TOTAL TIME: 25 MINUTES

4 ripe nectarines, pitted

3 large tomatoes

¼ cup finely chopped scallions

1 cup ice water

¼ cup fresh lime juice

¾ tsp salt

GARNISH: chopped fresh mint leaves

1. Purée 2 nectarines and 1½ tomatoes in food processor or blender. Dice remaining nectarines and tomatoes; stir into purée with remaining ingredients. Serve, or refrigerate up to 4 days.

2. Garnish servings with mint.

PER CUP: **67 cal, 2 g pro, 16 g car, 3 g fiber, 1 g fat (0 g sat fat), 0 mg chol, 259 mg sod**

Tuscan Tomato Soup & Parmesan Toasts

BLENDER OR FOOD PROCESSOR • OVEN • SERVES 4 • TOTAL TIME: 10 MINUTES

SOUP

1 jar (24 to 26 oz) marinara sauce

1 can (19 oz) cannellini beans, rinsed

1 jar (7 oz) roasted red peppers

2 Tbsp extra-virgin olive oil

1 clove garlic

1¾ cups water

¼ cup thin strips fresh basil leaves

Freshly ground pepper, to taste

PARMESAN TOASTS

12 thin slices French bread

12 tsp grated Parmesan cheese

1. SOUP: Put sauce, beans, peppers, oil and garlic in a blender or food processor; process until smooth. Pour into a medium saucepan along with the water. Stirring often, bring to a simmer over medium-high heat.

2. Remove from heat; stir in basil. Spoon into bowls; grind pepper on top.

3. PARMESAN TOASTS: Heat broiler. Line a baking sheet with foil. Place bread on foil; sprinkle each slice with 1 tsp grated Parmesan. Broil 2 to 3 minutes until lightly toasted.

PER SERVING **(without toasts): 296 cal, 11 g pro, 38 g car, 9 g fiber, 14 g fat (2 g sat fat), 0 mg chol, 1,596 mg sod**

Heirloom Tomato Gratin

SKILLET & OVEN • SERVES 10 • TOTAL TIME: 45 MINUTES

1 clove garlic, cut in half

3 Tbsp extra-virgin olive oil

1 large Vidalia onion, chopped

½ tsp grated orange zest

3 Tbsp fresh orange juice

2 tsp honey

1 Tbsp fresh thyme, chopped

4 lb mixed heirloom tomatoes, thickly sliced

½ tsp *each* salt and pepper

2 cups fresh bread crumbs

¼ cup grated Pecorino Romano cheese

1. Heat oven to 425°F. Vigorously rub inside of a shallow 2- to 2½-qt baking or gratin dish with garlic; discard garlic. Brush dish with 1 Tbsp oil to coat.

2. Heat 1½ Tbsp oil in a large skillet over medium-low heat. Add onion and cook 15 minutes, stirring often, just until translucent and tender, but not browned. Remove from heat; stir in orange zest and juice, honey and 1½ tsp thyme.

3. Scatter half over bottom of prepared dish; top with ½ the tomatoes and season with ½ the salt and pepper. Top with remaining onion mixture, tomatoes, salt and pepper, overlapping tomato slices to fit.

4. Mix bread crumbs, cheese and remaining ½ Tbsp oil and 1½ tsp thyme until crumbs are evenly moistened. Sprinkle over tomatoes.

5. Bake 20 to 24 minutes until crumbs are golden and juices bubble. Serve hot or warm.

PER SERVING: **130 cal, 3 g pro, 16 g car, 3 g fiber, 7 g fat (1 g sat fat), 2 mg chol, 204 mg sod**

Roasted Cauliflower & Onions

1 small head *each* purple, yellow, green and white cauliflower (about 5 lb total), cut in 1½-in. florets

3 large Vidalia onions, each cut lengthwise in 8 wedges

3 Tbsp extra-virgin olive oil

½ tsp *each* salt and pepper

½ cup pitted Kalamata olives, cut in slivers

¼ cup grated Parmesan cheese

2 Tbsp chopped Italian parsley

1. Heat oven to 475°F. Put cauliflower and onions, then oil, salt and pepper in a large, heavy-bottomed roasting pan; toss to mix and coat.

2. Roast 40 to 45 minutes, tossing vegetables every 15 minutes, until lightly charred and tender.

3. Add olives, Parmesan and parsley; toss to combine. Transfer to a large serving bowl. Serve hot, warm or at room temperature.

PER SERVING: **86 cal, 3 g pro, 10 g car, 3 g fiber, 5 g fat (1 g sat fat), 1 mg chol, 201 mg sod**

Corn & Leek Pudding

SKILLET & OVEN • SERVES 8 • TIME TOTAL: 1 HOUR

2 Tbsp butter

2 leeks, white and pale-green parts only, halved lengthwise, then thinly sliced crosswise (about 1 cup), rinsed well and drained

4 large eggs

½ cup heavy (whipping) cream

3 Tbsp cornstarch

2 Tbsp sugar

1 tsp vanilla extract

½ tsp salt

¼ tsp ground nutmeg

⅛ tsp ground red pepper (cayenne)

1 can (15¼ oz) whole-kernel corn, drained

1 can (14¾ oz) cream-style corn

¼ cup (1 oz) shredded Gruyère cheese

1. Heat oven to 350°F. Coat a shallow 1½-qt baking dish with nonstick spray.

2. Melt butter in a medium skillet on medium-high heat. Add leeks; sauté 3 minutes or until soft.

3. In a large bowl, whisk eggs, cream, cornstarch, sugar, vanilla, salt, nutmeg and cayenne until blended. Stir in leeks and whole and cream-style corn. Pour into prepared baking dish. Sprinkle with shredded cheese.

4. Bake, uncovered, 45 minutes or until top is golden and a knife inserted in center comes out clean. Let stand 10 minutes before serving.

PER SERVING: **231 cal, 7 g pro, 25 g car, 2 g fiber, 13 g fat (7 g sat fat), 138 mg chol, 454 mg sod**

PLANNING TIP: Can be baked up to 1 day ahead. Cool, cover and refrigerate. Bring to room temperature before reheating in microwave or a 350°F oven.

Scalloped Potatoes with Crumb Topping

OVEN • SERVES 10 • TOTAL TIME: 2 HOURS

2 Tbsp plus 1 tsp flour

3 cups nonfat milk

1½ cups shredded sharp Cheddar cheese

½ cup sliced scallions

1¼ tsp salt

¼ tsp pepper

6 large baking potatoes, rinsed well

¼ cup plain dried bread crumbs

2 tsp melted butter

1. Heat oven to 325°F. Grease a 13 x 9 x 2-in. baking dish.

2. Put flour in a medium saucepan. Slowly whisk in milk until blended, making sure to get into corners of pot. Bring to a boil over medium-high heat, stirring often. Reduce heat and simmer 2 to 3 minutes, stirring until thickened. Off heat, stir in 1 cup cheese, ¼ cup scallions and the salt and pepper.

3. Slice potatoes with a thin slicing disk of a food processor or ⅛-in. thick by hand (you should have 10 cups).

4. Put in prepared dish, add cheese sauce and toss to coat. Spread evenly and cover with foil. Bake 30 minutes.

5. Meanwhile, mix bread crumbs, butter and remaining ½ cup cheese in a small bowl until crumbs are evenly moistened.

6. Uncover baking dish, sprinkle with crumb mixture and bake uncovered 1 hour longer or until potatoes are tender and top is golden. Sprinkle with remaining scallions.

PER SERVING: **223 cal, 10 g pro, 30 g car, 3 g fiber, 7 g fat (4 g sat fat), 21 mg chol, 475 mg sod**

Potato-Rosemary Galette

SKILLET • SERVES 6 • TOTAL TIME: ABOUT 30 MINUTES

4 medium baking potatoes, peeled and submerged in a bowl of cold water to prevent browning

1 tsp crushed dried rosemary

1 tsp *each* salt and pepper

3 Tbsp butter

1. Pour water from bowl; dry potatoes with paper towels. Quickly shred using shredding disk of a food processor or the large holes of a 4-sided grater. Dry bowl; add potatoes, rosemary, salt and pepper; toss to mix.

2. Melt 2 Tbsp butter in a large nonstick skillet over medium-high heat until it stops foaming. Add potatoes, pressing them with a broad spatula into an even layer.

3. Cook 2 to 3 minutes, pressing down occasionally with spatula, until lightly browned on bottom. Dot top with remaining butter. Cover skillet, reduce heat to medium and cook 6 to 8 minutes until potatoes are tender when pierced.

4. Uncover and invert a large flat plate or baking sheet over skillet. Holding both together with oven mitts or potholders, carefully invert galette onto the plate. Slide galette back into skillet, increase heat to medium-high and cook 5 minutes or until browned on bottom. Slide onto serving plate, cut in wedges and serve immediately.

PER SERVING: **142 cal, 2 g pro, 21 g car, 2 g fiber, 6 g fat (4 g sat fat), 16 mg chol, 454 mg sod**

Rigatoni with Pesto & Chickpeas

FOOD PROCESSOR • SERVES 4 • TOTAL TIME: 20 MINUTES

12 oz rigatoni

1 can (19 oz) chickpeas, rinsed

¾ cup prepared basil pesto
(from a tub; see Note)

GARNISH: diced tomatoes and
Italian parsley, cut in narrow strips

1. Bring a large pot of lightly salted water to a boil. Add pasta and cook as package directs, reserving ½ cup cooking water.

2. Meanwhile, process ¾ cup chickpeas and the pesto in a food processor until smooth, scraping down sides as needed. Slowly pour reserved ½ cup pasta cooking water through feed tube; process until creamy.

3. Set a colander in kitchen sink; put the remaining chickpeas in the colander and drain the pasta. Return pasta and chickpeas to pot. Add pesto mixture and toss to mix and coat. Serve immediately, topping with tomatoes and parsley.

PER SERVING: **639 cal, 20 g pro, 81 g car, 6 g fiber,
26 g fat (4 g sat fat), 7 mg chol, 484 mg sod**

NOTE: Look for tubs of pesto in the dairy or fresh pasta section.

Penne with Mushroom "Bolognese"

FOOD PROCESSOR • SKILLET • SERVES 6 • TOTAL TIME: 20 MINUTES

1 lb penne rigate or other pasta

12 oz sliced shiitake mushroom caps

2 large garlic cloves

2 tsp olive oil

½ cup dry white or red wine (optional)

1 jar (26 oz) marinara sauce

½ tsp crushed dried rosemary

2 Tbsp chopped fresh parsley

SERVE WITH: grated Parmesan cheese

1. Bring a large pot of lightly salted water to a boil. Add pasta and cook as package directs.

2. Meanwhile, pulse mushrooms and garlic in food processor until finely chopped.

3. Heat oil in a large nonstick skillet. Add mushroom mixture; sauté over medium-high heat 3 minutes or until lightly browned.

4. Stir in wine (if using); boil 1 minute. Stir in sauce and rosemary, bring to boil, reduce heat and simmer 2 minutes to blend flavors. Stir in parsley; spoon onto pasta. Serve with Parmesan.

PER SERVING: **394 cal, 13 g pro, 72 g car, 5 g fiber, 7 g fat (1 g sat fat), 0 mg chol, 779 mg sod**

Orange-Spinach Pasta

SKILLET • SERVES 4 • TOTAL TIME: 15 MINUTES

2 navel oranges

¾ cup sliced scallions

1 cup fat-free half-and-half

12 oz capellini (angel-hair) pasta

2 bags (5 to 6 oz each) baby spinach

SERVE WITH: grated Parmesan cheese and crushed red pepper flakes

1. Bring a large pot of lightly salted water to a boil.

2. Meanwhile, finely grate the zest from 1 orange, then squeeze juice from both.

3. Bring orange juice and scallions to a simmer in a large nonstick skillet. Cook 3 minutes, or until juice is reduced to about 1 Tbsp. Add half-and-half and grated zest. Simmer 1 minute, then remove skillet from heat.

4. Stir pasta into pot of boiling water. Cook, stirring often, as package directs. Stir in spinach and cook 1 minute more or until pasta is firm-tender. Drain in a colander and return to pot. Add orange sauce; toss to mix and coat.

PER SERVING: 420 cal, 13 g pro, 85 g car, 7 g fiber, 1 g fat (0 g sat fat), 0 mg chol, 507 mg sod

Lite Fettucine Alfredo

SERVES 6 • TOTAL TIME: 20 MINUTES

1 lb spinach fettucine or linguine

1 Tbsp unsalted butter

2 garlic cloves, minced

3 Tbsp flour

2 cups fat-free half-and-half

¼ tsp *each* salt, pepper and ground nutmeg

¼ cup grated Parmesan cheese

1. Cook pasta in large pot of lightly salted boiling water as package directs.

2. Meanwhile, melt butter in a medium saucepan. Add garlic; cook over low heat 1 minute or until fragrant.

3. Whisk in flour, then slowly whisk in half-and-half until well combined. Whisk in salt, pepper and nutmeg, and bring to a boil, whisking frequently.

4. Reduce heat and simmer 5 minutes or until thickened. Remove from heat and stir in cheese until melted.

5. Drain pasta; return to pot. Add sauce and toss to mix and coat.

PER SERVING: **371 cal, 14 g pro, 65 g car, 3 g fiber, 6 g fat (3 g sat fat), 13 mg chol, 382 mg sod**

Caesar Spaghetti

SKILLET • SERVES 4 • TOTAL TIME: 27 MINUTES

12 oz spaghetti

2 Tbsp oil

½ cup plain dry bread crumbs

1 Tbsp minced garlic

1 vegetable-broth cube

1 lb head escarole, cut crosswise in strips (9 cups)

1 can (2 oz) flat anchovies, drained

5 plum tomatoes, cut in 1-in. chunks

⅓ cup grated Parmesan cheese

1. Bring a large pot of lightly salted water to a boil. Add pasta and cook as package directs.

2. Meanwhile, heat 1 Tbsp oil in a large nonstick skillet over medium-high heat. Add bread crumbs and cook 2 to 3 minutes, stirring often, until toasted. Pour into a medium bowl. Wipe out skillet.

3. Heat remaining 1 Tbsp oil in skillet over medium-high heat. Add garlic and sauté 1 minute or until fragrant. Add 1 cup water and broth cube. Cook, stirring to dissolve cube.

4. Add escarole, cover, and stirring once or twice, cook 3 minutes or until just wilted.

5. Drain pasta and return to pot. Add anchovies; toss with pasta until anchovies break up. Add escarole, broth and tomatoes; toss to mix and coat. Pour into serving bowl. Stir Parmesan into bread crumbs, sprinkle on pasta. Toss just before serving.

PER SERVING: **518 cal, 21 g pro, 81 g car, 6 g fiber, 12 g fat (3 g sat fat), 11 mg chol, 1,218 mg sod**

Risotto with Tomatoes & Caramelized Onions

SKILLET • SERVES 4 • TOTAL TIME: 37 MINUTES

2 Tbsp butter or margarine

2 medium onions, sliced

6 medium plum tomatoes, cut in bite-size pieces

2 boxes (6.1 or 5.7 oz each) onion-herb risotto mix or mushroom risotto mix

⅓ cup grated Parmesan cheese

1. Melt 1 Tbsp butter in a medium skillet over medium heat. Stir in onions, cover and cook 20 minutes, stirring occasionally, until onions are soft and golden brown. Uncover, stir in the tomatoes and cook about 2 minutes to heat through.

2. Meanwhile, put 4 cups water, the risotto mixes and remaining butter in a 2- to 3-qt saucepan. Bring to a boil, stirring occasionally. Reduce heat, cover and simmer 15 minutes or until rice is tender. Remove from heat; let sit covered 5 minutes.

3. Stir in onion-tomato mixture and sprinkle with Parmesan.

PER SERVING: **447 cal, 12 g pro, 79 g car, 5 g fiber, 9 g fat (3 g sat fat), 21 mg chol, 1,534 mg sod**

Pasta with Ratatouille

1 medium onion, chopped

3 garlic cloves, chopped

1 medium eggplant

3 medium zucchini

2 green bell peppers

6 plum tomatoes

1 can (8 oz) tomato sauce

1 Tbsp *each* chopped fresh oregano and thyme (or 1 tsp *each* dried)

½ tsp *each* salt and pepper

2 Tbsp *each* red wine vinegar and extra-virgin olive oil

1 lb rigatoni pasta

SERVE WITH: grated Parmesan cheese

1. Place onion and garlic in a 6-qt slow-cooker.

2. Cut eggplant, zucchini, peppers and tomatoes into 1-in. chunks; toss in large bowl with tomato sauce, herbs, salt and pepper. Add to slow-cooker.

3. Cook on low 5 to 8 hours until vegetables are tender. Stir in vinegar and oil.

4. Bring a large pot of lightly salted water to a boil. Add pasta and cook as package directs; toss with ratatouille. Serve with Parmesan.

PER SERVING: **360 cal, 12 g pro, 69 g car, 7 g fiber, 4 g fat (1 g sat fat), 0 mg chol, 256 mg sod**

Ravioli with Broccoli Rabe

SKILLET • SERVES 4 • TOTAL TIME: 17 MINUTES

2 pkg (9 oz each) refrigerated Four-Cheese Ravioli

12 oz broccoli rabe, rinsed and cut in bite-size pieces

2 cups marinara or Alfredo sauce

½ cup shredded part-skim mozzarella cheese

1. Fill a large skillet halfway with lightly salted water. Bring to a boil. Add ravioli; boil as package directs.

2. Meanwhile, place broccoli rabe in large bowl with ½ cup water. Cover, microwave until tender and drain.

3. Drain ravioli and return to skillet. Gently stir in sauce and broccoli rabe; heat through. Sprinkle with cheese; cover 1 minute or until cheese melts.

PER SERVING: **577 cal, 26 g pro, 76 g car, 9 g fiber, 18 g fat (10 g sat fat), 83 mg chol, 1,280 mg sod**

Eggplant Rollatini

1 jar (24 oz) puttanesca sauce

2 large eggplants

2 Tbsp oil

12 oz linguine fini

1. Heat oven to 400°F. Line 2 large baking sheets with nonstick foil.

2. Spread ½ cup puttanesca sauce in a 13 x 9-in. baking dish. Cut each eggplant lengthwise in 6 slices, trimming to make slices even. Brush both sides with oil. Place on baking sheets. Coarsely chop trimmings; add to sheets. Bake 20 minutes; turn and bake 10 minutes more or until tender.

3. Bring a large pot of lightly salted water to a boil. Add pasta and cook as package directs. Drain and return to pot. Stir chopped eggplant trimmings into remaining sauce, remove 1 cup sauce and reserve. Toss rest of sauce with the pasta.

4. Top each slice eggplant with ¼ cup pasta and roll up. Spread remaining pasta in baking dish; top with rollatini, seam side down. Spread with the 1 cup reserved sauce; cover with foil. Bake 30 minutes or until hot and bubbly.

PER SERVING: **340 cal, 11 g pro, 58 g car, 7 g fiber, 9 g fat (1 g sat fat), 0 mg chol, 507 mg sod**

Veggie-Stuffed Shells

SKILLET & OVEN • SERVES 6 • TOTAL TIME: 1 HOUR 5 MINUTES

1 box (12 oz) jumbo pasta shells

2 tsp olive oil

2½ cups chopped broccoli

1 cup shredded carrots

1 small onion, chopped

1 clove garlic, minced

1 box (10 oz) frozen leaf spinach, thawed and coarsely cut

¼ cup chopped fresh basil

1 cup lowfat small-curd cottage cheese (2%) or part-skim ricotta

2 Tbsp grated Parmesan cheese

¼ tsp *each* salt and pepper

1½ cups marinara sauce

½ cup shredded part-skim mozzarella cheese

1. Heat oven to 400°F. Bring a large pot of lightly salted water to a boil. Add pasta and cook as package directs. Drain and cool on baking sheet.

2. Meanwhile, heat oil in large skillet over medium-high heat. Sauté broccoli, carrots, onion and garlic 3 minutes or until just tender. Add spinach and ½ cup water; cover and cook 2 minutes or until vegetables are tender.

3. Remove cover; cook until liquid is mostly evaporated. Remove from heat; stir in basil, cottage cheese, Parmesan, salt and pepper. Spread marinara sauce on bottom of 13 x 9-in. baking dish.

4. Spoon 1 rounded Tbsp vegetable mixture into each shell; arrange in baking dish. Sprinkle with mozzarella, cover tightly with foil, and bake 35 minutes until hot and bubbly.

PER SERVING: **382 cal, 20 g pro, 60 g car, 7 g fiber, 8 g fat (3 g sat fat), 11 mg chol, 742 mg sod**

Three-Cheese Macaroni with Spinach

OVEN • SERVES 12 • TOTAL TIME: 55 MINUTES

4 Tbsp butter, plus extra for baking dish

1 cup chopped onion

⅓ cup flour

4½ cups milk

¼ tsp *each* salt and pepper

5 oz Gorgonzola cheese, broken in chunks

5 oz fontina cheese, rind removed, cut in chunks

1 cup grated Parmesan cheese

1 lb mini penne pasta

1 bag (6 oz) baby spinach

2 Tbsp plain dry bread crumbs

GARNISH: chopped parsley

1. Bring a large pot of lightly salted water to a boil. Heat oven to 375°F. Butter a shallow 3-qt baking dish or casserole.

2. Melt butter in a large saucepan over medium heat. Add onion and sauté 5 minutes until slightly softened but not browned. Whisk in flour; cook 2 minutes until blended. Slowly whisk in milk. Cook, whisking constantly, until mixture bubbles and thickens. Remove from heat; stir in salt, pepper, then Gorgonzola, fontina and ¾ cup Parmesan. Stir until cheese melts and sauce is smooth; set aside.

3. Stir pasta into boiling water. When water returns to a boil, cook 2 minutes less than time suggested on package. Drain well. Return pasta to pot, add spinach and cheese sauce and toss until spinach is wilted and pasta is evenly coated. Pour into prepared baking dish.

4. Mix rest of Parmesan with bread crumbs; sprinkle over top.

5. Bake about 30 minutes until browned on top. Cool 5 minutes before serving. Garnish with parsley.

PER SERVING: **380 cal, 17 g pro, 39 g car, 2 g fiber, 17 g fat (11 g sat fat), 53 mg chol, 685 mg sod**

PLANNING TIP: Prepare through Step 3 up to 1 day ahead. Refrigerate uncovered. Bring to room temperature before topping with crumb mixture and baking.

Creamy Macaroni & Cheese

SERVES 4 • TOTAL TIME: 30 MINUTES

12 oz wagon wheels, medium shells, elbow macaroni or other medium pasta shape

2 cups frozen chopped collard greens

1½ Tbsp butter or margarine

¾ cup fresh bread crumbs (see Note)

1 Tbsp grated Parmesan cheese

3 cups whole milk

⅓ cup flour

1½ cups shredded reduced-fat Cheddar cheese

¼ tsp *each* salt and paprika

1. Bring a large pot of lightly salted water to a boil. Add pasta and greens, and cook 10 to 12 minutes or until pasta and greens are tender; drain and return to pot.

2. Meanwhile, melt butter in a medium saucepan. Add bread crumbs and cook over medium-low heat, stirring often, 3 minutes or until golden and crisp. Remove to a small bowl; stir in Parmesan.

3. In same saucepan, whisk milk and flour until blended. Place over medium-high heat and bring to a boil, whisking often. Reduce heat and simmer uncovered 3 minutes until slightly thickened. Add Cheddar, salt and paprika. Stir over medium heat until cheese melts.

4. Add to pasta and greens in pot; toss to coat. Top servings with toasted crumbs.

PER SERVING: **676 cal, 35 g pro, 89 g car, 4 g fiber, 20 g fat (12 g saturated fat), 69 mg chol, 1,004 mg sod**

NOTE: To make bread crumbs, tear 2 slices white sandwich bread in pieces. Put in food processor; pulse until reduced to crumbs.

Cheesy Mexican Eggplant

OVEN • SERVES 6 • TOTAL TIME: 1 HOUR 20 MINUTES

2 eggplants, cut in ½-in.-thick rounds

Nonstick cooking spray

½ tsp freshly ground black pepper

2 cups marinara sauce

1 bottle (8 oz) taco sauce

½ tsp ground cumin

2 cups shredded Mexican-blend cheese

⅓ cup chopped cilantro

1½ cups white rice

1. Heat broiler. Place half the eggplant on a broiler rack, evenly coat with nonstick spray, then sprinkle with ¼ tsp pepper. Broil 4 in. from heat 4 to 8 minutes per side until lightly browned and tender. Repeat with remaining eggplant and pepper.

2. Heat oven to 350°F. In medium bowl, stir marinara and taco sauce with cumin.

3. Spread ½ cup sauce in a shallow 3-qt baking dish. Line with half the eggplant. Spoon on 1¼ cups sauce; top with 1 cup cheese and ¼ cup cilantro. Repeat layering with remaining eggplant, sauce and cheese; cover with foil.

4. Bake 40 minutes or until bubbly. Meanwhile, cook rice as package directs. Let eggplant rest 10 minutes. Sprinkle top with remaining cilantro. Serve with rice.

PER SERVING: **422 cal, 14 g pro, 57 g car, 6 g fiber, 15 g fat (9 g sat fat), 34 mg chol, 799 mg sod**

Eggplant-Polenta Stacks

SKILLET • SERVES 4 • TOTAL TIME: 30 MINUTES

1 Tbsp plus 2 tsp olive oil

1 small eggplant, halved and sliced

¾ cup chopped onion

2 small zucchini, sliced

¼ cup sliced sun-dried tomatoes

¼ tsp *each* salt and pepper

1 tube (16 to 18 oz) ready-to-heat polenta, cut into 8 slices

1 large tomato, cut into 8 slices

½ cup shredded part-skim mozzarella cheese

1 cup marinara sauce, heated in microwave

GARNISH: chopped fresh basil

1. Heat 1 Tbsp of the oil in a large, deep nonstick skillet. Add eggplant and onion. Cover and cook over medium-high heat 4 minutes, stirring a few times until slightly softened.

2. Add 1 tsp of the remaining oil, the zucchini, sun-dried tomatoes, salt and pepper. Cover and cook 6 to 7 minutes, stirring often, until vegetables are tender. Remove to bowl; wipe or rinse skillet.

3. Heat remaining 1 tsp oil in skillet. Add polenta; cook 2 minutes over medium-high heat until bottoms are golden.

4. Off heat, turn polenta and spoon the vegetable mixture onto polenta (it's OK if some falls onto the skillet). Top each with 1 slice of tomato and sprinkle with cheese.

5. Place skillet over low heat; cover and cook 2 minutes or until cheese melts. Sprinkle with basil, if desired, and serve with sauce.

PER SERVING: **282 cal, 9 g pro, 39 g car, 6 g fiber, 10 g fat (3 g sat fat), 9 mg chol, 948 mg sod**

Orange-Soy Tofu Stir-Fry

¾ cup water

1 tsp grated orange zest

¼ cup fresh orange juice

2 Tbsp lite soy sauce

1½ tsp cornstarch

¼ tsp crushed red pepper flakes

2 tsp canola oil

1 pkg (14 oz) lowfat extra-firm tofu, patted dry, cut into 1-in. cubes

2 tsp *each* minced garlic and fresh ginger

1 bunch asparagus, bottoms trimmed, cut in pieces

2 medium red bell peppers, sliced

1 cup frozen shelled edamame

1 pkg (3.5 oz) sliced shiitake mushrooms

½ cup sliced scallions

GARNISH: toasted sesame seeds

1. Mix water, zest, juice, soy sauce, cornstarch and red pepper flakes in a cup.

2. Heat 1 tsp oil in a large nonstick skillet. Add tofu; cook over high heat 5 minutes, turning often, until golden. Add garlic and ginger. Reduce heat and cook 30 seconds. Spoon tofu mixture into a bowl.

3. Heat 1 tsp oil in skillet. Add asparagus, peppers, edamame and mushrooms; stir-fry 5 minutes.

4. Add orange juice mixture and bring to a boil. Stir in tofu and scallions; toss. Garnish with toasted sesame seeds.

PER SERVING: **295 cal, 23 g pro, 24 g car, 6 g fiber, 13 g fat (2 g sat fat), 0 mg chol, 306 mg sod**

Spring Vegetable Frittata

SKILLET • SERVES 6 • TOTAL TIME: 34 MINUTES

3 medium carrots, shredded

1 lb asparagus, bottoms trimmed (see Note), cut in pieces

1 Tbsp oil, preferably olive

6 cups frozen country-style hash brown potatoes

1 tsp salt

8 large eggs, beaten with a fork

1½ cups shredded smoked Gouda or mozzarella cheese

½ cup sliced scallions

1. Bring 1 cup water to a boil in a large nonstick skillet. Add carrots and asparagus; reduce heat, cover and simmer 5 to 6 minutes until asparagus are crisp-tender. Drain well; wipe out skillet.

2. Heat oil in skillet over medium heat. Add potatoes, sprinkle with ½ tsp salt and cook 5 minutes or until bottoms are lightly browned. Turn with a spatula and press down, pushing some potatoes up the sides of the skillet.

3. Mix remaining ½ tsp salt with the eggs; pour mixture over potatoes. Top with the carrots and asparagus. Cover and cook over medium-low heat 10 minutes or until eggs are almost set.

4. Sprinkle with cheese and scallions, cover and cook 2 to 3 minutes to melt cheese.

PER SERVING: **311 cal, 19 g pro, 20 g car, 3 g fiber, 17 g fat (7 g sat fat), 323 mg chol, 827 mg sod**

NOTE: Hold asparagus with both hands near bottom end. Bend each spear until it breaks and discard the woody end.

Stovetop Spinach & Swiss Cheese Strata

SKILLET & OVEN • SERVES 5 • TOTAL TIME: 30 MINUTES

6 large eggs

1½ cups milk

¼ tsp *each* salt and freshly ground black pepper

1¼ cups shredded Swiss cheese

2 Tbsp butter

1 small onion, chopped

5 slices firm white bread, cut into 1-in. cubes

1 pkg (10 oz) frozen chopped spinach, thawed and squeezed dry

GARNISH: chopped tomato

1. Beat eggs, milk, salt and pepper in medium bowl. Stir in 1 cup cheese.

2. Melt butter in 10-in. deep nonstick skillet over medium-high heat. Add onion and sauté 2 minutes until softened. Add bread cubes and cook, stirring, 3 minutes or until bread is lightly browned. Reduce heat to low and stir in spinach. Pour egg mixture evenly into skillet. Cover and cook 10 minutes or until egg mixture is just set.

3. Meanwhile, preheat broiler. If skillet handle is not ovenproof, wrap in foil. Sprinkle with remaining cheese. Broil 4 in. from heat, 1 to 2 minutes until lightly browned. Scatter tomato on top.

PER SERVING: **406 cal, 23 g pro, 31 g car, 3 g fiber, 22 g fat (11 g sat fat), 298 mg chol, 636 mg sod**

Italian Lentil & Vegetable Stew

SLOW-COOKER • SERVES 5 • TOTAL TIME: 8 TO 10 HOURS ON LOW

1½ cups dried lentils

3 cups butternut squash, cut in 1-in. chunks

2 cups bottled marinara sauce

2 cups green beans, ends trimmed and beans cut in half

1 red bell pepper, cut in 1-in. pieces

1 large all-purpose potato, peeled and cut in 1-in. chunks

¾ cup chopped onion

1 tsp minced garlic

1 Tbsp olive oil, preferably extra-virgin

SERVE WITH: grated Parmesan cheese

1. Mix lentils and 3 cups water in a 3-qt or larger slow-cooker. In a large bowl, mix remaining ingredients except olive oil; place over lentils.

2. Cover and cook on low 8 to 10 hours until vegetables and lentils are tender. Stir in the oil. Serve in soup plates or bowls. Serve Parmesan in a bowl separately.

PER SERVING: **383 cal, 21 g pro, 66 g car, 12 g fiber, 7 g fat (1 g sat fat), 0 mg chol, 644 mg sod**

Curried Red Lentils

1 Tbsp oil

1 medium onion, chopped

2 tsp chopped garlic

2 tsp red curry powder

1 can (14 oz) vegetable broth

1 can (13.5 oz) lite coconut milk
(not cream of coconut)

1 bag (16 oz) red lentils, picked over
and rinsed

3 cups fresh cauliflower florets

1 red bell pepper, seeded and
coarsely chopped

1 medium zucchini, cut in
¾-in. pieces

¼ cup chopped fresh cilantro

1. Heat oil in large pot over medium heat. Add onion; sauté 4 minutes or until translucent. Add garlic and curry powder; cook 1 minute.

2. Stir broth, coconut milk and ½ cup water into saucepan. Bring to a boil. Add lentils, cauliflower, pepper and zucchini. Cover and reduce heat.

3. Return to a simmer, cover and cook, stirring once, 10 to 12 minutes until lentils and vegetables are just tender. Stir in cilantro.

PER SERVING: **424 cal, 29 g pro, 65 g car, 39 g fiber, 8 g fat (3 g sat fat), 0 mg chol, 125 mg sod**

Serve with rice for a hearty main dish.

No-Hurry Vegetable Curry

SLOW-COOKER • SERVES 6 • TOTAL: 6 TO 7 HOURS ON LOW

1 can (14 oz) light coconut milk

¼ cup flour

1½ Tbsp red curry paste

1 large onion, chopped

4 small Yukon gold potatoes, halved

4 cups butternut squash, cut in 1½-in. chunks

4 cups cauliflower florets

1 can (15 oz) chickpeas, rinsed

1 red bell pepper, cut in 1-in. pieces

1 cup frozen peas

3 cups cooked basmati rice

GARNISH: chopped cilantro

1. Whisk coconut milk, flour and curry paste in a 3½-qt or larger slow-cooker. Stir in vegetables except peas; mix well.

2. Cover and cook on low 6 to 7 hours until vegetables are tender. Stir in peas, cover and let sit 5 minutes. Serve with rice; garnish with cilantro.

PER SERVING: **355 cal, 11 g pro, 63 g car, 10 g fiber, 7 g fat (3 g sat fat), 0 mg chol, 244 mg sod**

Veggie Chili

5½ cups water

¾ cup bulgur wheat

2 tsp olive oil

1 cup *each* chopped onion and red bell pepper

2 Tbsp salt-free chili powder

2 tsp *each* minced garlic and ground cumin

1 large can (28 oz) crushed tomatoes

1 can (15 oz) 100% pure pumpkin

1 medium zucchini, diced

1 cup frozen corn

1 can (15½ oz) low-sodium black beans, rinsed

½ cup chopped cilantro

ACCOMPANIMENTS: reduced-fat Cheddar cheese, reduced-fat sour cream

1. Put 3 cups water and bulgur in a medium microwave-safe bowl. Cover and microwave on high until bulgur is tender, about 15 minutes.

2. Meanwhile, heat oil in a large nonstick skillet. Add onion and pepper; sauté 5 minutes. Add chili powder, garlic and cumin; sauté until fragrant.

3. Add remaining water, the tomatoes, pumpkin, zucchini and corn; bring to a boil over medium-high heat. Reduce heat and simmer 10 minutes, stirring occasionally, until vegetables are tender.

4. Stir in beans and bulgur; heat through. Remove from heat, stir in cilantro.

PER SERVING: **266 cal, 12 g pro, 52 g car, 14 g fiber, 3 g fat (1 g sat fat), 0 mg chol, 249 mg sod**

Photo Credits

Page 6: Charles Schiller; page 9: Anastassios Mentis; page 11: John Uher; page 14: Mary Ellen Bartley; page 17: John Uher; page 18: Jacqueline Hopkins; page 21: Charles Schiller; page 23: John Blais; page 24: Alison Miksch; page 27: Jacqueline Hopkins; page 31: Dasha Wright; page 32: Mark Thomas; page 34: Anastassios Mentis; page 35: Ann Stratton; page 36: Mary Ellen Bartley; page 39: Mark Thomas; page 41: Mary Ellen Bartley; page 44: Anastassios Mentis; pages 46, 49: Charles Schiller; page 50: Shaffer Smith; page 53: Charles Schiller; page 54: Sang An; page 56: Jacqueline Hopkins; page 59: John Uher; page 60: Jeff McNamara; page 63: Jim Franco; page 66: Mary Ellen Bartley; page 67: Charles Schiller; page 69: Mary Ellen Bartley; page 70: Jim Franco; page 72: Charles Schiller; page 75: Wendell Webber; page 77: Mary Ellen Bartley; page 78: John Uher; page 81: Jim Franco; page 82: Anastassios Mentis; page 84: Mark Thomas; page 85: Wendell Webber; page 87: Anastassios Mentis; page 88: Jacqueline Hopkins; page 91: Lucas Allen; pages 92, 95: Kate Sears.